2022 FIFA WORLD CUP
Things to Know About 2022 World Cup in Qatar

Copyright

Table of content

Chapter 1

Things to Know About 2022 World Cup in Qatar
The ongoing year's World Cup will be not typical for another in a couple of perspective.

Curiously, the best event in football history, the FIFA World Cup, is to be worked with by an Arab country this year. The beginning up will start with a shocking match among Senegal and The Netherlands on 21st November at the Lusail Stadium in Qatar. The clarification the opposition is being held fairly later is a direct result of Qatar's outrageous temperatures during the common mid year months during the cup is routinely held

The 2022 event in Qatar will offer a ton of firsts for the world's most prominent soccer rivalry. There is another region featuring new fields, likewise another spot on the timetable.

This is just the resulting World Cup set in Asia, joining the 2002 event in South Korea and Japan, and the essential in the Middle East.

Among central areas, Europe has worked with the most World Cups in history with 11. South America has worked with five, North America has worked with three and Africa has worked with one.
First winter World Cup in Northern Hemisphere
Sports.
As a result of Qatar's pre-summer heat, the opposition was moved from its run of the mill spot in the timetable to a November start. It will be the key World Cup that doesn't occur in May, June or July.

Most expensive World Cup in history
Qatar as far as anyone knows is spending more than $200 billion on structure,

including field improvement, for the 2022 World Cup. By relationship, the 2018 World Cup as far as anyone knows cost Russia some place in the scope of $10 and $15 billion, making Qatar the most expensive World Cup to date.

All World Cup fields in Qatar in somewhere near one hour of each other
Players won't have to go out far to move between various settings at the 2022 World Cup.

All of the eight World Cup fields in Qatar are in something like one hour of driving detachment from each other. While accommodating, it comes from how Qatar is more unobtrusive than each U.S. state beside Delaware and Rhode Island.

Last World Cup with 32 gatherings
The World Cup is stretching out in 2026.

The event, which will be held in the United
States, Canada and Mexico, is the first in
World Cup history that will feature 48 teams.
In turn, the 2022 competition in Qatar will be
the seventh and final World Cup with a
32-team format.

- trophyGetty
- World Cup
- England
- Argentina
- Brazil
- Spain
- Belgium
- France
- Portugal
- Qatar
- Mexico
- Netherlands
- Denmark
- Germany

- Atlético Uruguay
- Switzerland
- United States
- Croatia
- Senegal
- Iran
- Japan
- Morocco
- Serbia
- Poland
- Korea Republic
- Tunisia
- Cameroon
- Canada
- Ecuador
- Saudi Arabia
- Ghana

The initiation is on to an overall show-stopper in Qatar, with 32 nations arranged to start seeking after down the most phenomenal honor in worldwide football

Four extra year cycle is basically over as players, guides and partners from each side of the planet begin to count during the opportunity to the 2022 World Cup in Qatar.

There will be 32 nations expecting to seek after down overall wonderfulness in the Middle East, with there a ton of forceful gatherings that acknowledge they can mimic the undertakings from 2018 of reigning champions France.

Simply a solitary will win, but there commitments to be a ton of surges and spills on the way and you can view all that you need as acquainted with each possible step of that journey here courteousness of GOAL.

Where is World Cup 2022 being held and at which fields?
Lusail Iconic Stadium General ViewGetty Images

History is being made in 2022 as the World Cup finals head to the Middle East strangely.

The event will in like manner be happening across November and December, rather than its standard June/July opening, due to the taking off summer temperatures in Qatar and will be done in a united 28-day plan.

An energetically expected challenge will get rolling on November 21 and will see move made in across eight exceptionally gathered settings in five metropolitan networks, with the Lusail Iconic Stadium playing host to the keep going on December 18.

When was the draw made for World Cup 2022?
The draw for the World Cup finals happened at the Doha Exhibition and Convention Center on April 1.

Carli Lloyd, Jermaine Jenas and Samantha
Johnson were nearby to oversee events in
Qatar, with assistance given by any similarity
to Cafu (Brazil), Lothar Matthaus (Germany),
Adel Ahmed MalAllah (Qatar), Ali Daei
(Iran), Bora Milutinovic (Serbia/Mexico), Jay
Okocha (Nigeria), Rabah Madjer (Algeria)
and Tim Cahill (Australia).

The 29 nations that had recently qualified at
that stage were, close by three spots assigned
to play-off clear victors, put into four pots
considering FIFA's overall situating structure.

Which gatherings have prepared for World Cup 2022?

Canada celebrate 2022

There were at this point three spots accessible
to anybody when the finals draw happened,
with one of the UEFA portion end of the time
games being deferred until June in view of
Ukraine being not ready to take in forceful

devices following Russia's assault of their lines.

Two between confederation end of the time games were moreover anticipated mid-June, with nations propelling down AFC, CONMEBOL, CONCACAF and OFC portions drew in with those difficulties.

What are the social occasions for World Cup 2022?
Kylian Mbappe France 2022Getty Images
As is by and large the circumstance in events, for instance, this, the finals draw flung a great deal of enchanting subplots to what is currently shaping doing be a momentous wearing blockbuster.

The amazing 'Social occasion of Death' will see Spain and Germany conflicting in 2022, with there some serious quality on show in that little affiliation.

Group A	Group B
Qatar	England
Ecuador	Iran
Senegal	United States
Netherlands	Wales

Group C	Group D
Argentina	France
Saudi Arabia	Australia
Mexico	Denmark
Poland	Tunisia

Group E	Group F

Spain	Belgium
Costa Rica	Canada
Germany	Morocco
Japan	Croatia

Group G	**Group H**
Brazil	Portugal
Serbia	Ghana
Switzerland	Uruguay
Cameroon	South Korea

Chapter 2

***What are the World Cup 2022 contraptions
and get going times?***

World Cup 2022 will get going on November
21, with has Qatar helping with opening
things up.

A movement squeezed pack stage will run
until December 2, when 16 sides will make
their way through to the knockout rounds.

The last-16 mechanical assemblies are a
result of happen between December 3-6, with
the quarter-finals being held tight December
9 and 10.

Semi-last showdowns with a ton being
referred to are made arrangements for
December 13 and 14, with the last pulling in
an overall horde of billions on December 18 -

the day after a third spot play-off has seen bronze beautifications circulated.

What is the World Cup 2022 match ball?
Adidas has conveyed 'Al Rihla', the power match roll of the 2022 World Cup in Qatar ●

Adidas uncovered the power World Cup 2022 match ball, known as 'Al Rihla' on March 30.

Al Rihla signifies 'the outing' in Arabic, with the ball setup drawing inspiration from Qatar's uncommon designing, "renowned" boats and public standard.

The Al Rihla is said to move speedier in the air than any of the past World Cup balls and purportedly gives "the main degree of accuracy and reliability on the field of play".

The 20 sheets of the ball are integrated to help with redesigning smoothed out highlights, helping players with dealing with the precision and steer of their shots, while the thing is made totally from water-based inks and glues - a first for a World Cup model.

Franziska Loeffelmann, plan boss in the football delineations and hardwear division at Adidas, has offered a summary of the key components.

She said: "The game is getting faster, and as it speeds up, precision and flight strength ends up being essentially critical. The new arrangement allows the ball to stay aware of its speed basically higher as it adventures through the air."

The full overview of gatherings that have prepared for World Cup 2022 can be found under.

The full list of teams that have qualified for World Cup 2022 can be found below.

Team	Association
Qatar	AFC
Brazil	CONMEBOL
Belgium	UEFA
France	UEFA
Argentina	CONMEBOL
England	UEFA
Spain	UEFA
Portugal	UEFA
Mexico	CONCACAF

Netherlands	UEFA
Denmark	UEFA
Germany	UEFA
Uruguay	CONMEBOL
Switzerland	UEFA
United States	CONCACAF
Croatia	UEFA
Senegal	CAF
Iran	AFC
Japan	AFC

Morocco	CAF
Serbia	UEFA
Poland	UEFA
South Korea	AFC
Tunisia	CAF

Cameroon	CAF
Canada	CONCACAF
Ecuador	CONMEBOL
Saudi Arabia	AFC
Ghana	CAF
Australia	AFC
Costa Rica	CONCACAF
Wales	UEFA

World Cup 2022: Full schedule list
Group stage

Monday, November 21:

Group A – Senegal v Holland, 10am

Group B – England v Iran, 1pm

Group A – Qatar v Ecuador, 4pm

Group B – USA v Wales, 7pm

Tuesday, November 22:

Group C – Argentina v Saudi Arabia, 10am

Group D – Denmark v Tunisia, 1pm

Group C – Mexico v Poland, 4pm

Group D – France v Australia, 7pm

Wednesday, November 23:

Group F – Morocco v Croatia, 10am

Group E – Germany v Japan, 1pm

Group E – Spain v Costa Rica, 4pm

Group F – Belgium v Canada, 7pm

Thursday, November 24:

Group G – Switzerland v Cameroon, 10am

Group H – Uruguay v South Korea, 1pm

Group H – Portugal v Ghana, 4pm

Group G – Brazil v Serbia, 7pm

Friday, November 25:

Group B – Iran v Wales, 10am

Group A – Qatar v Senegal, 1pm

Group A – Holland v Ecuador, 4pm

Group B – England v USA, 7pm

Saturday, November 26:

Group D – Tunisia v Australia, 10am

Group C – Poland v Saudi Arabia, 1pm

Group D – France v Denmark, 4pm

Group C – Argentina v Mexico, 7pm

Sunday, November 27:

Group E – Japan v Costa Rica, 10am

Group F – Belgium v Morocco, 1pm

Group F – Croatia v Canada, 4pm

Group E – Spain v Germany, 7pm

Monday, November 28:

Group G – Cameroon v Serbia, 10am

Group H – South Korea v Ghana, 1pm

Group G – Brazil v Switzerland, 4pm

Group H – Portugal v Uruguay, 7pm

Tuesday, November 29:

Group A – Holland v Qatar, 3pm

Group A – Ecuador v Senegal, 3pm

Group B – Wales v England, 7pm

Group B – Iran v USA, 7pm

Wednesday, November 30:

Group D – Tunisia v France, 3pm

Group D – Australia v Denmark, 3pm

Group C – Poland v Argentina, 7pm

Group C – Saudi Arabia v Mexico, 7pm

Thursday, December 1

Group F – Croatia v Belgium, 3pm

Group F – Canada v Morocco, 3pm

Group E – Japan v Spain, 7pm

Group E – Costa Rica v Germany, 7pm

Friday, December 2:

Group H – South Korea v Portugal, 3pm

Group H – Ghana v Uruguay, 3pm

Group G – Cameroon v Brazil, 7pm

Group G – Serbia v Switzerland, 7pm

Round-of-16

Saturday, December 3:

Match 49 – 1A v 2B – Khalifa International Stadium, 3pm

Match 50 – 1C v 2D – Al Rayyan Stadium, 7pm

Sunday, December 4:

Match 52 – 1D v 2C – Al Thumama Stadium, 3pm

Match 51 – 1B v 2A – Al Bayt Stadium, 7pm

Monday, December 5:

Match 53 – 1E v 2F – Al Janoub Stadium, 3pm

Match 54 – 1G v 2H – Ras Abu Aboud Stadium, 7pm

Tuesday, December 6:

Match 55 – 1F v 2E – Education City Stadium, 3pm

Match 56 – 1H v 2G – Lusail Stadium, 7pm

Quarter-finals

Friday, December 9:

Match 57 – Winner of Match 49 v Winner Match 50 – Lusail Stadium, 7pm

Match 58 – Winner of Match 53 v Winner
Match 54 – Education City Stadium, 3pm

Saturday, December 10:

Match 59 – Winner Match 51 v Winner
Match 52 – Al Bayt Stadium, 7pm

Match 60 – Winner Match 55 v Winner
Match 56 – Al Thumama Stadium, 3pm

Semi-finals

Tuesday, December 13:

Match 61 – Winner Match 57 v Winner
Match 58 – Lusail Stadium, 7pm

Wednesday, December 14:

Match 62 – Winner Match 59 v Winner
Match 60 – Al Bayt Stadium, 7pm

Third-place play-off:

Saturday, December 17:

Match 63 – Khalifa International Stadium,
3pm

Final

Sunday, December 18:

Match 64 – Lusail Stadium, 3pm